BLACK BEAUTY

'What more could I want?' says Black Beauty, as he describes his pleasant home and his kind owners. 'Freedom! For the first four years of my life I had a large field where I could gallop around at full speed – with no straps, no bit, and no blinkers. Now I stood in a stable, night and day, except when I was wanted for work.'

In the 1870s there was plenty of work for horses – pulling carriages and cabs and carts through crowded cities, along country roads, in all kinds of weather.

Black Beauty has been well trained. He knows that he must never bite or kick or run away, and must always do what he is told, however tired or hungry he feels. He always behaves well, but when he is sold, first to one owner, then another, and another, he learns how hard a horse's life can be, and how stupid and how cruel some people are . . .

OXFORD BOOKWORMS LIBRARY
Human Interest

Black Beauty

Stage 4 (1400 headwords)

Series Editor: Jennifer Bassett
Founder Editor: Tricia Hedge
Activities Editors: Jennifer Bassett and Christine Lindop

ANNA SEWELL

Black Beauty

Retold by
John Escott

Illustrated by
Sally Wern Comport

OXFORD UNIVERSITY PRESS

OXFORD
UNIVERSITY PRESS

Great Clarendon Street, Oxford OX2 6DP

Oxford University Press is a department of the University of Oxford.
It furthers the University's objective of excellence in research, scholarship,
and education by publishing worldwide in

Oxford New York

Auckland Cape Town Dar es Salaam Hong Kong Karachi
Kuala Lumpur Madrid Melbourne Mexico City Nairobi
New Delhi Shanghai Taipei Toronto

With offices in

Argentina Austria Brazil Chile Czech Republic France Greece
Guatemala Hungary Italy Japan Poland Portugal Singapore
South Korea Switzerland Thailand Turkey Ukraine Vietnam

OXFORD and OXFORD ENGLISH are registered trade marks of
Oxford University Press in the UK and in certain other countries

ISBN 978 0 19 479166 3

A complete recording of this Bookworms edition of
Black Beauty is available on audio CD ISBN 978 0 19 479148 9

Typeset by Wyvern Typesetting Ltd, Bristol

Printed in Hong Kong

Illustrated by: Sally Wern Comport/Shannon Associates

Word count (main text): 15,400 words

For more information on the Oxford Bookworms Library,
visit www.oup.com/elt/bookworms

CONTENTS

My first home

The first place I can remember well was a pleasant field with a pond of clear water in it. Trees made shadows over the pond, and water plants grew at the deep end. On one side was another field, and on the other side we looked over a gate at our master's house, which stood by the roadside. At the top of our field were more tall trees, and at the bottom was a fast-running stream.

While I was young, I lived on my mother's milk, but as soon as I was old enough to eat grass, my mother went out to work during the day and came back in the evening.

There were six other young horses in the field, although they were older than I was. We all galloped together round

The first place I remember was a pleasant field.

the field, and had great fun. But sometimes the others would kick and bite.

'They are young farm horses and haven't learned how to behave,' my mother told me. 'You are different. Your father is well known, and your grandfather twice won the most important race at Newmarket. Your grandmother was quiet and gentle, and you have never seen me kick or bite, have you? I hope you will grow up to be gentle and a willing worker, and never bite or kick.'

I have never forgotten my mother's advice. She was a clever and sensible old horse. Her name was Duchess, but our master often called her Pet. He was a good, kind man, and my mother loved him very much. Whenever she saw him at the gate, she trotted across. He used to pat her and say, 'Well, old Pet, and how is your little Darkie?' I was a dull black colour, so he called me Darkie. He sometimes brought a piece of bread for me, or a carrot for my mother, and I think we were his favourites.

When I was two years old, something happened which I have never forgotten. It was early spring, and there was a light mist over the trees and fields. I and the other young horses were feeding at the lower end of the field when we heard the distant cry of dogs.

The oldest among us lifted his head to listen. 'There are the hounds!' he said, and immediately raced off. The rest of us followed him to the top of the field, where we could see several fields beyond.

My mother and another old horse were standing near.

'They've found a hare,' said my mother, 'and if they come this way, we shall see the hunt.'

Soon the dogs were all racing down the field next to ours, making a loud 'yo–yo–yo–yo!' sound at the top of their voices. After them came men on horses, some in green coats, and all galloping as fast as they could. Suddenly, the dogs became silent and ran around with their noses to the ground.

'They've lost the smell of the hare,' said the old horse. 'Perhaps it will escape.'

But the dogs began their 'yo–yo–yo–yo!' again and came at full speed towards our field. Just then a hare, wild with fear, ran towards the trees. The dogs jumped over the stream and ran across the field, followed by the huntsmen. Six or eight jumped their horses over the stream, close behind the dogs. Before the hare could get away, the dogs were upon her with wild cries.

A hare, wild with fear, ran towards the trees.

We heard a terrible scream, and that was the end of the hare. One of the men picked her up and held her by the leg. She was covered in blood, but all the huntsmen seemed pleased.

I was so greatly surprised that at first I did not see what was happening by the stream, but when I did look, I saw a sad sight. Two fine horses were down, one in the stream and the other on the grass. One rider, who seemed unhurt, was climbing out of the water, but the other lay quite still.

'His neck is broken,' said my mother. 'I can't understand why men are so fond of this sport. They quite often hurt themselves and ruin good horses, all for one hare that they could get more easily some other way. But we are only horses, and don't know why men do these things.'

They carried the dead rider to our master's house, and I heard afterwards that it was George Gordon, the only son of a local landowner, and a fine young man.

A man from the village came to look at the black horse on the grass. The animal was in great pain and one of his legs was broken. The man began to feel the horse all over, then he shook his head. Someone ran to our master's house and came back with a gun. Soon after, there was a loud bang and a terrible cry, then all was still. The black horse did not move again.

My mother was very unhappy. 'I've known that horse for years,' she said. 'His name was Rob Roy. He was a good brave horse.' She never went near that end of the field again.

Not many days after, we heard the church bell and saw a long, strange black carriage, pulled by black horses. They were taking the body of young George Gordon to the churchyard to bury him. He would never ride again. I never knew what they did with Rob Roy, but it was all for one little hare.

— 2 —

Birtwick Park

I was beginning to grow handsome. My coat was fine and soft, and was a shiny black. I had one white foot, and a pretty white star on my forehead. When I was four years old, Mr Gordon came to look at me. He looked closely at my eyes, my mouth, and my legs, and then I had to walk and trot and gallop for him.

'When he has been trained,' Mr Gordon said to my master, 'he will do very well.'

My master liked to train his horses himself before selling them, and the next day my training began.

I had a pretty white star on my forehead.

To train a horse is to teach him to wear a saddle, and to carry a man, woman or child on his back. The horse must also learn to wear a collar, and to stand still when it is put on; then to have a carriage fixed behind him, and to go fast or slow, whichever his driver wishes. He must never bite or kick or talk to other horses, and must always do what his master tells him, however tired or hungry he feels.

Like all horses that have grown up, I had to wear a bit and bridle. A bit is a great piece of cold hard metal, as thick as a man's finger, which is pushed into a horse's mouth between his teeth and over his tongue, with the ends coming out at the corners. It is held there by straps which go over the horse's head, under his neck, round his nose and under his chin. Reins, which the rider holds, are fastened to each end of the bit. Slowly, with my master's kind words and gentle ways, I learned to wear my bit and bridle.

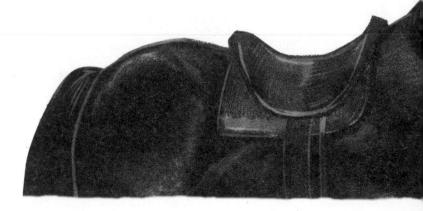

Next there was the saddle. My master put it on my back very gently, then fixed the straps under my body, speaking quietly to me all the time. Then one morning, he got on my back and rode me round the field on the soft grass. He did this every day until I was used to it. Then he took me to the village where a man fixed metal shoes on to each hoof. My feet felt heavy and strange, but I got used to this, too.

There were more new things to wear. First, a heavy collar on my neck, and a bridle with great side pieces against my eyes, called blinkers. With these on, I could only see in front of me. But in time I got used to everything, and could do my work as well as my mother.

For a fortnight, my master sent me to a neighbour's farm for another kind of training, which was very useful to me. One field was next to the railway and had sheep and cows in it, and I was put in among them.

I had to wear a bit and bridle, and a saddle.

7

A man fixed metal shoes on to each hoof.

I shall never forget the first train that thundered by, and how I galloped to the far side of the field, trembling with fear at this terrible noise. But after a few days I cared as little as the sheep and cows when a train passed by.

It was early in May when a man came to take me away to Mr Gordon's house. My master said, 'Goodbye, Darkie. Be a good horse, and always do your best.' I put my nose into his hand and he patted me kindly, and then I left my first home.

* * *

Mr Gordon's house, which was called the Hall, stood in Birtwick Park, near the village. We went into the Park through a large gate, then trotted along a smooth road between some trees to the house and gardens. Beyond this were the stables.

There was room for many horses and carriages. My

8

stable had four good stalls and a large window. It was very pleasant. The first stall was called a loose box, where a horse is not tied up all the time but is free to move around as he likes. It is a great thing to have a loose box. The groom put me into it and gave me some oats. Then he patted me, spoke kindly, and went away. In the stall next to mine stood a little fat grey pony.

'Hello,' I said. 'What is your name?'

'Merrylegs,' he said, turning round. 'I'm very handsome. I carry the young ladies on my back, and sometimes I take Mrs Gordon out in one of the carriages. Are you going to live next to me in the box?'

'Yes,' I said.

'Then I hope you are well-behaved,' he said. 'I don't like anyone who bites.'

A horse's head looked over from the stall beyond. It was a tall brown mare, and she did not look pleased. 'So it's you who has turned me out of my box,' she said.

In the next stall stood a little fat grey pony.

9

'I'm sorry,' I said, 'but the man put me in here, so it is not my fault. I don't want to argue with anyone; I just wish to live in peace.'

Later, Merrylegs told me about the tall brown mare.

'Ginger has a bad habit of biting people,' he explained. 'One day, she bit James in the arm, and Miss Flora and Miss Jessie, the children, were afraid to come into the stable after that. If you don't bite, I hope they'll start to come again.'

I told him I never bit anything except grass and could not understand why Ginger bit people.

'No one was ever kind to her before she came here,' said Merrylegs. 'John and James do all they can to please her, and our master is never unkind. I'm twelve years old, and I know that there isn't a better place for a horse all round the country than this. John has been here fourteen years and is the best groom there ever was. And you never saw a kinder stableboy than James. There was no reason for Ginger to bite anyone. It's her own fault that she did not stay in the box.'

The name of the groom was John Manly. The next morning, he got out his brushes and gave me a good grooming, then put a saddle on me. He rode me slowly at first, then at a trot, then at a gallop. As we came back through the Park, we met Mr and Mrs Gordon. They stopped and John jumped off.

'Well, John, how does he go?' said Mr Gordon.

'He's a fine horse, sir,' said John. 'He's fast, but the lightest touch of the rein will guide him. They were shooting birds near Highwood, and a gun went off close by. He pulled up a little, but I just held the rein and he wasn't frightened at all. It's my opinion he was never frightened or beaten when he was young.'

'Good,' said Mr Gordon. 'I'll ride him tomorrow.'

I remembered my mother's advice, and the next day I tried to do exactly what my master wanted me to do. He was a very good rider, and when he came home his wife was waiting for him at the door.

'How do you like him, my dear?' she asked.

'I have never ridden a more pleasant horse,' answered Mr Gordon. 'What shall we call him?'

'What about Blackbird, like your uncle's old horse?' said his wife.

'He's far handsomer than Blackbird,' said Mr Gordon.

'Yes,' she said, 'he's quite a beauty, and he has a kind, intelligent face. Shall we call him Black Beauty?'

'Black Beauty – why, yes, I think that's a very good name,' said Mr Gordon.

John went into the stable and told James.

'I'd call him Rob Roy,' said James, 'if it did not remind everyone of the past. I never saw two horses more alike.'

'That's not surprising,' said John. 'Didn't you know that Farmer Grey's old Duchess was the mother of them both?'

So poor Rob Roy who was killed at the hunt was my brother! Now I understood why my mother was so unhappy when he died.

John was very proud of me, and seemed to know just

how a horse feels. And James was kind, too.

A day or two later, I went out in the carriage with Ginger. I wondered how we would get on together, but I found it easy to trot along beside her.

Merrylegs was a happy little pony and was everyone's favourite. We were soon great friends and I became quite happy in my new home.

— *3* —

Ginger's story

*W*hat more could I want? Freedom! For the first four years of my life I had a large field where I could gallop around at full speed – with no straps, no bit, and no blinkers. Now I stood in a stable, night and day, except when I was wanted for work, and sometimes when John took me out, I felt so strong, so full of life, that I wanted to jump or dance.

'Calm down, boy!' he would say.

Then, as soon as we were out of the village, he would let me trot fast for a few miles. Some grooms punished a horse for getting too excited, but not John. He knew how to control me with only the sound of his voice, and I was very fond of him.

Sometimes we did have our freedom in the field for an hour or two. This was on fine Sundays in the summer,

I went out in the carriage with Ginger.

because the carriage never went out on Sundays. It was wonderful. The grass was cool and soft to our feet, and the air was so sweet. And we could gallop or lie down or roll over on our backs, or do what we liked.

One day Ginger asked me about my old home and my training. When I finished telling her, she said, 'Life has been different for me. I was taken from my mother when I was young, and there was no kind master like yours to look after me. I had a bad time when I was trained. Several men caught me in a corner of the field and one held my nose so hard that I could only just breathe. Then another pulled my mouth open to put the bit in, and I was pulled along and beaten from behind. They didn't give me a chance to understand what they wanted.

'The old master, Mr Ryder, knew about horses, but he gave up most of the business to his son, who was tall and strong, but not gentle. They called him Samson, and he said that no horse could throw him out of the saddle. One day, he made me run round the field on a long rein until I was

We could lie down or roll over on our backs.

very tired and miserable. The next morning he did the same again, then he put a saddle and bridle on me, and a new kind of bit into my mouth.

'The new bit was very painful and I pulled away and stood up on my back legs, which made him very angry. He stayed in the saddle and beat me with a whip, but after a long and terrible battle I threw him off and galloped to the other end of the field.

'He beat me with a whip.'

'I watched him go into the stable, but no one came to fetch me. Time went on and the sun was very hot. I was hungry and very thirsty. At last, just as the sun was going down, the old master came out with some oats. He spoke kindly and held out the oats for me to eat, then patted me gently and looked at the blood on my sides where Samson had whipped me.

'"Poor girl!" he said, then led me to the stable. Samson was there. "Keep out of the way," said the master. "You've done a bad day's work for this horse with your bad temper. A bad-tempered man will never make a good-tempered horse." He led me into my box and took off my saddle and bridle. Then he called for some warm water and gently cleaned the blood from my sides.

'After that, he often came to see me, but a man called Joe went on training me. He was quiet and thoughtful and I soon learned what he wanted.

'After my training,' Ginger went on, 'I was bought by a dealer to match another horse of my colour. But then we were sold to a man in London who drove us with a bearing rein – a rein to hold our heads up unnaturally high and to keep them there, for hours and hours, until the pain was terrible. We had to wear two bits instead of one, and mine was so sharp that it made my mouth bleed. Sometimes we waited for hours while our master or mistress was at parties or the theatre, and if we weren't patient, the driver would whip us.'

'Didn't your master care about you at all?' I said.

'Only about how we looked,' replied Ginger. 'He knew very little about horses. The driver told him I had a bad temper but would soon get used to the bearing rein. I was willing to work and learn, but they were so cruel that it made me angry. Then I broke away from the carriage one day, and that was the end of that place.

'I was sold to another man, but he had a groom as bad-tempered as Samson. He hit me across the legs with his stable brush if I didn't move quickly. I hated him, and one day when he made me angry, I bit him! He never came into my stall after that, and I was soon sold again.

'A dealer heard of me and said he thought he knew one place where I should do well. "It's wrong for a fine horse to go bad like that," he said. And I was brought here, not long before you came. Of course, it's very different here. But who knows how long it will last? I've decided that all men are my natural enemies.'

I was sorry for Ginger, but as the weeks went on, she became happier and more gentle.

'I do believe Ginger is getting quite fond of me,' James said one day.

'She'll be as good as Black Beauty one day,' replied John. 'Kindness is all she needs, poor thing!'

— *4* —

Kindness and cruelty

A neighbour of the Gordons', Mr Blomefield, had a large family of boys and girls who often came to play with Miss Jessie and Miss Flora. One of the girls was the same age as Miss Jessie, two of the boys were older, and there were several little ones. Whenever they came, the children loved to ride Merrylegs.

One afternoon when they were visiting, James brought Merrylegs in and said, 'Now, behave yourself.'

'What did you do, Merrylegs?' I asked him.

'Those young people didn't seem to know when I was tired,' he said, 'so I just threw them off backwards. It was the only thing they could understand.'

'You threw the children off!' I said. 'Oh, no! Did you throw Miss Flora or Miss Jessie?'

'No, of course not! I'm quiet and careful with them, and

with the little ones. I'm the best friend and riding teacher those children have. It's not them, it's the boys,' he said. 'The other children rode me for nearly two hours, then the boys rode me, one after the other, for an hour, hitting me with a stick. I didn't get annoyed but I did get tired, so I stopped once or twice to let them know. But boys think a horse is like a machine and can go on as long and as fast as they want it to. They never think that we get tired. As one was whipping me, I stood up on my back legs and he fell off. He got on again and I did the same. Then the other boy tried and I put *him* down on the grass. They're not bad boys, and don't mean to be cruel, but they have to learn.

'When they told James, he was angry to see those big sticks and told the boys not to use them again.'

'I would give those boys a good kick,' said Ginger.

'I know you would,' said Merrylegs. 'But they expect me to look after those children, and they expect me to be good-tempered, and I will be. You never had a place where they were kind to you, Ginger, and I'm sorry for you. But good places make good horses, and I wouldn't make our people angry for anything! If I started kicking people, they would very quickly sell me, perhaps to someone cruel. I hope that never happens.'

* * *

I often wondered why Sir Oliver, the oldest horse in the stable, had so short a tail – only about twenty centimetres long – and one day I asked him, 'Did you have an accident?'

'It was no accident!' he said, angrily. 'My long and

Merrylegs stood up on his back legs and the boy fell off.

beautiful tail was cut off when I was a young horse. At that time, some owners thought it was fashionable!'

'How terrible!' I said.

'Yes, terrible and cruel,' said Sir Oliver. 'Now I can never brush the flies off my sides or back legs, and all because of fashion. Some owners cut off the tails of their dogs to make them look brave, or cut their pretty little ears to make them look fashionable. They don't cut off the ends of their *children's* ears, do they? Why do they think it's all right to do these things to their animals?'

Mr Gordon was never cruel, and he would not stand by and watch others be cruel to animals. We were riding home one morning when we saw a big man driving towards us in a small carriage, pulled by a beautiful little pony. As he got to the Park gates, the pony turned towards them. Without warning, the man pulled the pony's head round so roughly that the little animal almost fell over. Then he began to whip the pony, angrily. The animal tried to move forward, but the man held it back and continued to whip it.

'Sawyer!' shouted my master.

The man looked up. He was a builder who often came to the Park to do work. 'He's too fond of going his own way!' he told my master. 'He's not supposed to turn in through your gates; the road is straight on.'

'You often drive that pony to my house,' said my master. 'It only shows that the horse is intelligent and remembers these things. How could he know you weren't going there today? I've never seen a horse beaten so cruelly or with so much anger. What will people think of you, Sawyer? As well as hurting the horse, you hurt your own good name – do you want people to think of you as a cruel, bad-tempered man?'

We went home slowly, and I could tell by his voice that the master was unhappy at what we had seen.

— 5 —

The storm

One day in the autumn my master had to go to a distant town on business. John harnessed me to the carriage and the three of us went off. There had been a lot of rain, and the wind was very strong. When we came to the river, the water was so high it nearly reached the wooden bridge, and many of the fields were under water. In one low part of the road the water was half-way up to my knees.

We got to the town and the master's business took a long time. It was late in the afternoon when we started back for home. The wind was much stronger, and as we drove through a wood, I heard my master say, 'I've never been out in a storm as bad as this, John.' Indeed, I thought so too, hearing the terrible noise of that wild wind in the trees.

'I wish we were out of this wood,' said my master.

'Yes, sir,' agreed John. 'We don't want one of those branches coming down on top of us.'

But just as he finished speaking, there was a great noise of wood breaking, and a big tree came crashing down through the other smaller trees and fell across the road right in front of us! I was very frightened and I stopped immediately, but I didn't turn round or try to run away. John jumped out and quickly ran to my side.

'What can we do now, John?' said my master.

'We can't drive over the tree or get round it, sir,' said John. 'We'll have to go back to the crossroads, and take the longer road round to the wooden bridge. It will make us late, but the horse isn't tired.'

It was nearly dark when we got to the wooden bridge. We could see water over the middle of it, but this often happened when the river was high. But the moment my feet touched the first part of the bridge, I was sure something was wrong, and I stopped suddenly.

'Go on, Beauty,' said my master, and he touched me with the whip. I did not move, so he hit me sharply, but I would not go forward.

'There's something wrong,' said John, and he jumped from the carriage and began to look round. He tried to lead me forward. 'Come on, Beauty, what's the matter?'

Of course I could not tell him, but I knew the bridge was not safe.

Just then a man ran out of the house on the other side of the bridge. 'Stop! Stop!' he cried.

'What's the matter?' shouted my master.

'The bridge is broken in the middle,' said the man, 'and

I was sure something was wrong.

part of it was carried away. If you come across, you'll fall in the river!'

'Thank you, Beauty!' John said to me, and turned me gently round to the right-hand road by the riverside.

It got darker and the wind got quieter as I trotted towards home by another, much longer road. The two men were quiet for some time, but then my master spoke.

'We were very close to drowning in that river, John,' he said. 'Men may be clever enough to think of things for themselves, but animals know things *without* thinking, and that's often saved a man's life, as it has ours tonight. People don't realize how wonderful their animals are, nor do they make friends with them as they should.'

When we arrived back at Birtwick Park, the mistress ran out to meet us. 'I've been so worried!' she said. 'Are you all right? Did you have an accident?'

'We nearly did,' said my master. 'But Black Beauty was cleverer than we were, and saved us all from drowning!'

* * *

One morning early in December, the master came to the stable with a letter in his hand, looking very serious.

'Good morning, John,' he said. 'Tell me, does James work hard and do what you tell him to do?'

'Yes, sir, always,' replied John.

'And he doesn't stop work when your back is turned?'

'Never, sir.'

'And if he goes out with the horses, does he stop to talk to friends, or go into houses where he has no business, leaving the horses outside?' said the master.

'No, sir,' said John. 'And if anybody has said that about James, I don't believe it. I never had a pleasanter, more honest young man in this stable.'

The master smiled and looked across at James, who was standing by the door. 'James, I'm glad John's opinion of you agrees with my own,' he said. 'I've had a letter from my wife's brother, Sir Clifford Williams. He wants me to find him an honest young groom who knows what he's doing. The man who drives his carriage is getting old and needs a young man who will work with him and be able to do his job one day. How old are you?'

'Nineteen next May, sir,' said James.

'That's young. What do you think, John?'

'It *is* young, sir,' said John, 'but he's tall and strong. He doesn't have much experience of driving, but he has a light touch and a quick eye.'

'Well, James,' said the master, 'talk to your mother at dinner-time and let me know what you want to do.'

A few days later it was agreed that James would go to Clifford Hall in a month or six weeks, and for the next few weeks he drove the carriage. We went in and out of town, through busy streets, and to the railway station, where the road was narrow and there were lots of other carriages hurrying to and from the station.

Then my master and mistress decided to visit some friends who lived about seventy-five kilometres from our home. 'You can drive us, James,' said my master.

The fire

The first day we travelled about fifty kilometres, but James drove carefully and made sure that Ginger and I were always on the smoothest part of the road. It was evening when we reached the hotel where we were going to stay that night. It was in the Market Place and two stablemen came out to us.

The chief stableman was a pleasant old man, and he led me into a long stable with six or eight stalls in it, and two or three horses. The younger man brought in Ginger, and James watched while we were groomed.

'I thought I was quick,' James told the old stableman, 'but you're quicker than anyone.'

'I've worked with horses since I was twelve years old, and I can tell you it's good to be able to work with a well-behaved, well-cared for animal like this,' said the stableman, patting my neck. 'Who is your master?'

'Mr Gordon of Birtwick Park,' said James.

'I've heard of him,' said the stableman. 'He's a good judge of horses, and the best rider in this part of the country.'

'He doesn't ride very often now,' said James, 'not since the poor young master was killed.'

'I read about that in the newspaper,' said the stableman. 'A fine horse was killed too, wasn't it?'

26

'Yes, an excellent horse,' said James. 'He was the brother of this one, and just like him.'

'Terrible!' said the old man. 'It was a bad place to jump, wasn't it? A man's life and a horse's life are worth more than a hare – or they should be!'

Later that evening, the younger stableman brought in another horse, and a young man with a pipe in his mouth came into the stable to talk to him.

'Towler, go up and get some hay and put it down for this horse, will you?' said the stableman. 'But put down your pipe first.'

'All right,' said the other man, and went up a ladder and through a little door. I heard him step across the floor over my head and push down some hay through a hole in the roof, into the new horse's feeding place.

James came in to look at us before he went to bed, and then the door was locked.

I don't know how long I slept, or what time it was when I woke up, but the air seemed thick and I heard Ginger and another horse moving about worriedly. It was quite dark and I could see nothing. The stable was full of smoke, and it was almost impossible to breathe.

The smoke seemed to come from the little door above me, and I could hear a strange noise up there. The other horses were now all awake, moving about restlessly.

At last I heard someone outside, and then the younger stableman ran in with a light. He began to untie the horses, and tried to lead them out. The first horse would not go with him, nor the second or third. He tried to pull me out, but he was so frightened himself that he frightened me, and I would not move.

The noise above was louder now and there was a shout of 'Fire!' outside. The old stableman came in quietly and quickly and got one horse out, then another. By now the flames were coming down through the roof and the noise was terrible.

Then I heard James's voice, quiet and friendly as it always was. 'Come on, Beauty,' he said, 'we'll soon get you out of this smoke.' He took off his scarf and tied it over my eyes, then led me out, patting me all the time. He took the scarf off, then shouted, 'Take this horse, somebody, while I go back for the other!'

Windows in the hotel were open and people were shouting. I watched the stable door, where the smoke came out thicker than ever. Then I heard one voice above all the others, and recognized it as my master's.

'James Howard! James Howard! Are you there?'

There was no answer, only the crash of something falling in the stable – but the next moment I saw James coming through the smoke, leading Ginger with him.

'My brave boy!' said the master. 'Are you hurt?'

James shook his head, unable to speak because of the smoke.

Suddenly, I heard the sound of wheels and galloping horses. 'It's the fire-engine!' shouted someone.

Two horses ran past me, pulling the heavy fire-engine.

James led me out, patting me all the time.

The firemen jumped out, and we went quickly into the wide, quiet Market Place, out of their way.

The master led us to a large hotel on the other side where a stableman came to take us in; then the master hurried off to find his wife.

The next morning, he came to see how we were and to speak to James. I did not hear much, but James looked very happy and the master looked proud of him.

How did the fire start? Someone said they saw Dick Towler go into the stable smoking a pipe, but that when Dick came out he didn't have it. The young stableman said that he asked Dick to go up the ladder to put down some hay, but also told him to put down his pipe first. Dick said that he did this, but nobody believed him.

James said the roof and floor had all fallen in and only the black walls were standing; the two poor horses who could not get out were buried under the fallen roof.

— 7 —

Joe Green

The rest of our journey was very easy, and the next evening we reached the house of our master's friend, where a groom took us to a comfortable stable. We stayed two or three days, then returned home. John was glad to see us, and we were glad to see him.

'I wonder who will come in my place,' said James.

'Little Joe Green,' said John. 'He's only fourteen and a half but he has a kind heart and wants to come, so I've agreed to try him for six weeks.'

The next day, Joe Green came to learn all he could before James left. He was a nice happy boy and always came to work singing. But then the day came when James had to leave us.

'I'm leaving a lot behind,' he said sadly to John. 'My mother, and you, a good master and mistress, and the horses. And I shan't know anybody at the new place.'

'It's hard to leave your home for the first time,' said John, 'but if you get on well – which I'm sure you will – your mother will be proud of you.'

Everyone was sorry to lose James, but Joe tried hard to learn, and John was pleased with him.

* * *

One night I woke up to hear the stable bell ringing loudly. I heard the door open at John's house, and his feet running up to the Hall. He was back quickly.

'Wake up, Beauty!' he said, coming into the stable. 'We must go quickly now!' And before I could think, he had the saddle on my back and the bridle on my head.

The master was waiting at the Hall door with a letter in his hand. 'Ride for your life, John!' he said. 'Give this to Dr White, then rest your horse and be back as soon as you can. Mrs Gordon is very ill.'

Away went John and I, through the Park, through the

village, and down the hill. There was a long piece of flat road by the riverside, and John said, 'Now Beauty, do your best!' I needed no whip, and for two miles I galloped as fast as I could – perhaps even faster than my grandfather, who won the race at Newmarket. When we came to the bridge, John slowed me down a little and patted my neck. 'Well done, Beauty!' he said.

Then I was off again, as fast as before. The air was cold and the moon was bright, and it was a pleasant night. We went through a village, then a dark wood, then uphill, then downhill, and after twelve kilometres, we came to the town.

It was three o'clock when we stopped by Dr White's door. John rang the bell, then knocked on the door like thunder. A window was pushed up and Dr White's head appeared. 'What do you want?' he said.

'Mrs Gordon is very ill,' said John. 'You must come at once, or she'll die. Here's a letter.'

The doctor was soon at the door. 'My horse has been out all day and is exhausted. Can I take yours?'

'My master told me to rest him,' said John, 'but take him if you think it's best, sir.'

'I'll soon be ready,' said the doctor.

John stood by me and patted my neck. I was very hot. Then the doctor came out with his riding whip.

'You won't need that, sir,' said John. 'Black Beauty will go until he drops.'

The doctor was a heavier man than John, and not so

Then I was off again, as fast as before.

good a rider, but I did my very best. Joe was waiting at the
gate and the master was at the Hall door. He did not say a
word. The doctor went into the house with him, and Joe
led me to the stable.

My legs were shaking and there was not a dry hair on my
body. The water ran down my legs and I was hot all over.
Poor Joe! He was young and knew very little. He did the
best he could, cleaning my legs and my chest, but he did not
put a warm cloth on me; he thought I was so hot that I
would not like it. He gave me some cold water to drink,
then he gave me some food and went away.

Soon I began to shake and tremble with cold, and I ached

33

all over. I wished John was there, but he had twelve kilometres to walk, so I tried to sleep.

After a long time, I heard John at the door. I gave a low cry, and he was at my side in a moment. I could not tell him how I felt, but he seemed to know immediately. He covered me with three warm cloths, then ran for some hot water and made me a warm drink.

John seemed very angry. 'Stupid boy!' he said to himself, over and over again. 'No cloth put on, and I suppose the water was cold too. Boys are no good!'

I became very ill, and could not breathe without pain. John looked after me day and night, and my master often came to see me too.

'My poor Beauty,' he said one day. 'My good horse, you saved your mistress's life. Yes, you saved her life.'

I was very glad to hear that. John told my master that he never saw a horse go so fast.

One night, Tom Green, Joe's father, came to help John give me my medicine, then stayed for a while. At first both men were silent, then Tom said, 'John, please say a kind word to Joe. The boy is heart-broken; he can't eat his meals, and he can't smile. He knows it's his fault Beauty is ill, but he did his best. He says if Beauty dies, no one will ever speak to him again. But he's not a bad boy.'

After a short pause, John said, 'I know he meant no harm, but I'm proud of that horse, and I hate to think his life may be thrown away like this. But I'll give the boy a kind word tomorrow, if Beauty is better.'

I heard no more of this conversation, as the medicine did well and sent me to sleep, and in the morning I felt much better.

Joe learned quickly after this, and was so careful that John began to give him many things to do. One day, John was out and the master wanted a letter taken immediately to a gentleman's house about five kilometres away. He told Joe to saddle me and take it.

The letter was delivered and we were returning through a field where we saw a cart full of bricks. They were so heavy that the wheels of the cart were half-buried in the soft ground, and the horses could not move the cart at all. The man leading the horses was shouting and whipping them without stopping.

'Don't whip the horses like that,' Joe shouted at him. 'The wheels are half-buried and won't move. I'll help you take some bricks out to make the cart lighter.'

'Mind your own business!' said the man angrily. He was in a terrible temper and more than half-drunk.

Joe turned me, and we galloped towards the house of the brickmaker, Mr Clay. Joe knocked on the door.

The door opened. 'Hallo, young man,' began Mr Clay.

'There's a man in your field whipping two horses to death!' Joe told him, his voice shaking with anger. 'I told him to stop, but he wouldn't. I offered to help him lighten the cart, but he refused. I think he's drunk. Please go, sir!'

'I will!' said the man, and hurried off.

When we got home, Joe told John all about it.

35

'Don't whip the horses like that,' Joe shouted.

'You did the right thing,' said John. 'Many people would ride by and say it was none of their business. But cruelty is everybody's business.'

Just before dinner, the master sent for Joe. The drunken man was accused of cruelty to horses and Joe was wanted to tell his story to the police.

'I'll tell it gladly,' said Joe.

We heard afterwards that the poor horses were so exhausted and so badly beaten that the man might have to go to prison.

Joe came across and gave me a friendly pat. 'We won't allow cruelty, will we, old friend?' he said.

And he seemed to have grown up suddenly.

— *8* —

Earlshall Park

I lived at Birtwick Park for three happy years, but then changes came. Our mistress was often ill and the doctor advised her to go and live in a warm country for two or three years. Everyone was very sorry, but the master immediately started making arrangements to leave England.

John did his work silently and sadly, and Joe didn't sing any more. Then we heard that the master had sold Ginger and me to an old friend of his, Lord Gray. Merrylegs was given to the neighbour, Mr Blomefield, and Joe was employed to look after him. John was offered several good jobs but he wanted to wait and look around.

'I want to train young horses,' he told the master.

'I cannot think of anyone more suitable for that work than you, John,' said the master. 'If I can help you in any way, write to me.'

The next morning, John took Ginger and me to Earlshall Park where Lord Gray lived. There was a very fine house and lots of stables. John asked for Mr York, who was going to be our new driver.

Mr York was a good-looking man of about forty, with a voice that expected to be obeyed. He called a groom to take us to our boxes, then invited John to have a drink with him. We were taken to a pleasant stable and put in boxes next to one another, then we were groomed and fed. Half an hour later, John and Mr York came to see us.

Mr York looked at us carefully. 'Is there anything you want to mention about them, Mr Manly?' he said.

'I don't believe there's a better pair of horses in the country,' said John, 'but they're not alike. The black one has the most perfect temper I've ever known. The other was badly treated before she came to us, but has grown better-tempered in the last three years. We've never used a bearing rein with either of them.'

'They'll wear one here,' said York. 'Lady Gray follows the fashion, and if her horses are not reined up tight, she doesn't like it.'

'I'm sorry to hear that,' said John. He came to pat each of us for the last time. I held my face close to him, which was all I could do to say goodbye. And then he was gone, and I have never seen him since.

Lord Gray came to look at us the next day and seemed pleased. He heard what John had said about us. 'Keep an on the mare,' he said to York. 'Don't make the bearing rein too tight at first, and I'll mention it to my wife.'

In the afternoon, we were harnessed to the carriage and Lady Gray came out and looked at us. She was a tall, proud-looking woman and did not look pleased, but she said nothing and got into the carriage.

The bearing rein annoyed me but did not pull my head any higher than I was used to carrying it. I was worried about Ginger, but she seemed quite happy.

But the next afternoon when Lady Gray came down the steps, she said, 'York, you must put those horses' heads higher; they don't look nice.'

'I'm sorry, my Lady,' said York, 'but they have not been reined up for three years. But if it pleases you, I can take them up a little more.'

'Do that,' she said.

That day we had to pull the carriage up a steep hill. I wanted to put my head forward to make the work easier, but I couldn't.

'Now you can see what it's like,' said Ginger, when we came back. 'If it doesn't get any worse, I shall say nothing. But I won't have the rein pulled up tight!'

Each day the bearing reins were shortened a little more; then one day Lady Gray came out later than usual and said, 'York, when will you get those horses' heads up? Pull them up at once, and let's have no arguing.'

York came to me first and made the rein very tight. Then he went to Ginger. But the moment he took off the rein in order to shorten it, she stood up on her back legs. York and the groom could not control her. She kicked herself out of the carriage and fell down, kicking me on the leg as she went. York sat on her head to keep her still and shouted, 'Let the black horse out! Undo the carriage! Cut the harness!'

Ginger kicked herself out of the carriage.

The groom cut me out of the harness and hurried me back to my box, then ran back to York. I was angry and my leg hurt, and I felt that I wanted to kick the first person who came near me.

Soon after, Ginger was led in by two grooms. York was with her and came to look at me.

'I knew those bearing reins would cause trouble,' he said to himself. He saw where I had been kicked and washed the place gently with hot water to help the pain.

Lord Gray was angry when he heard what had happened. He blamed York for taking orders from the mistress, and York said that he would take orders only from Lord Gray himself from now on. But things went on the same as before, except that Ginger was never put into the carriage again. I pulled it with a horse called Max who was used to the tight rein. But those four months pulling Lady Gray's carriage were terrible. The sharp bit cut into my tongue and mouth, the rein hurt my neck and made it difficult to breathe, and I felt tired and very miserable.

In the spring, Lord Gray and some of his family went up to London and took York with them. Two daughters remained at the Hall. Lady Harriet never went out in the carriage, and Lady Anne preferred riding on horseback with her brother or cousins. She chose me for her horse and I enjoyed these rides, sometimes with Ginger, sometimes with Lizzie, a horse liked by the young gentlemen.

There was a gentleman called Blantyre staying at the Hall, who always rode Lizzie and was so pleased with her that Lady Anne wanted to try her.

'I don't advise it,' said Blantyre. 'She's too easily frightened for a lady to ride.'

'My dear cousin,' said Lady Anne, laughing, 'I've been riding horses since I was a baby and have followed the hounds many times. Now, help me up.'

So Blantyre helped her into the saddle, then climbed on me. Just as we were moving off, Lady Harriet asked for a message to be taken to Dr Ashley in the village.

The village was about two kilometres away, and the doctor's house was the last one in it. Blantyre got off to open the gate for Lady Anne but she said, 'I'll wait here for you.'

He went off and we waited.

There was a field with an open gate on the opposite side of the road, and at that moment some young horses came trotting out. They were wild and excited, and there was a boy behind them, waving a large whip. Suddenly, one of the young horses ran across the road, and banged into Lizzie's back legs. She gave a violent kick, nearly unseating Lady Anne, and immediately galloped away at full speed.

I gave a loud neigh for help and made a noise with my feet until Mr Blantyre came running out of the doctor's house. He saw Lizzie and Lady Anne, now far away down the road, and quickly jumped into the saddle, and we raced after them.

For about two kilometres the road was straight, then it d to the right before becoming two roads. Long before we came to the bend, Lady Anne was out of sight. Which way had she gone? A woman was in her garden, looking up the road. 'Which way?' shouted Blantyre.

'To the right!' cried the woman.

Away we went, up the right-hand road. We saw her for a moment, then she was gone again round another bend. Several times we saw her, but lost her again. Then we came to some rough land, very uneven and full of holes in the ground – the worst possible place for galloping.

On this open ground we could now see Lady Anne clearly, her long hair flying out behind her in the wind, and slowly we began to catch up. There was a wide ditch ahead and I was sure it would stop them, but without a pause Lizzie jumped it – and fell.

I cleared the ditch and landed safely. Lady Anne was lying on the ground, not moving. Blantyre jumped down beside her and called her name, but there was no reply. Her face was white and her eyes were closed.

'Annie, dear Annie, do speak!' he cried.

There were two men cutting grass close by and they saw Lizzie galloping away without a rider and came across.

'Can you ride?' Blantyre asked one of them.

'I'm not a good horseman, sir,' he said. 'But I'll do my best.'

'Ride this horse to the doctor's and ask him to come immediately, then go on to the Hall,' said Blantyre. 'Tell them all you know and ask them to send a carriage.'

The man climbed into my saddle and we galloped off. I

'Annie, dear Annie, do speak!' he cried.

tried not to shake him about too much, and he soon discovered that he needed no whip.

There was a lot of excitement at the Hall when they heard what happened. I was put into my box, the saddle and bridle were taken off and a cloth was thrown over me.

Two days later, Blantyre came and patted me.

'You did well,' he said. 'I'm sure you knew Annie was in danger. She must ride only you from now on.'

From this I knew that my young mistress was out of ∙er and would soon be able to ride again.

9

The accident and new masters

A man called Reuben Smith looked after us while York was in London. He was gentle and clever with horses, and an excellent driver. But he had one fault – he sometimes drank too much. For weeks or months he was all right, but then without warning he would begin to drink heavily and behave badly. But he was a useful man so York had kept quiet about Smith's drinking, saying nothing to Lord Gray. Then one night Smith drove some ladies and gentlemen home from a party and was so drunk that he could not hold the reins. York could not hide this and Lord Gray told Smith to leave.

However, some time later, York spoke again to Lord Gray, who was very kind-hearted, and he took Reuben Smith back. Smith promised never to get drunk again and kept his promise, and because of this he was told to look after the stables while York was away.

One day the carriage needed some repairs so it was arranged that Smith would take it to town, leave it at the carriage-maker's, and then ride me back again. Mr Blantyre wanted to go to the station, so he went with us.

At the station, Mr Blantyre gave Smith some money and said, 'Take care of Lady Anne, Reuben, and don't let anyone else except her ride Black Beauty.'

We left the carriage at the maker's, and Smith rode me to

the White Lion hotel. He told the stableman to give me some food and have me ready for four o'clock. One of my front shoes was loose but the stableman did not see it until four o'clock. Smith came back at five and said he would now leave at six because he'd met some old friends. The stableman told him about the loose shoe.

'It'll be all right until we get home,' said Smith.

He finally came back at nine o'clock, shouting loudly and in a very bad temper. We left and almost immediately he began to gallop, often giving me sharp cuts with the whip, although I was going at full speed. Before we were out of the town my shoe came off, but Smith was too drunk to notice.

It was very dark, and on the rough road at that speed, my foot was soon cut and bleeding from the sharp stones. I could not go on; the pain was too great, and I fell violently on both my knees. Smith was thrown off. He tried to get up but couldn't, then he lay still.

I could do nothing but wait.

It was nearly midnight when I heard a horse's feet and the wheels of a carriage. I neighed loudly, and was very happy to hear an answering neigh from Ginger, and men's voices. Then the carriage came out of the darkness and stopped.

Two men jumped down beside Smith. 'It's Reuben,' said one, 'and he's not moving, Robert.'

'He's dead,' said Robert, touching Smith. 'His hands are and his head is covered with blood.'

'He's dead,' said Robert, touching Smith.

They looked at me and saw my cut knees.

'The horse has been down and thrown him!' said Robert. He tried to lead me forward but I almost fell again. 'He's bad in the foot, too. No wonder he went down, riding over these stones without a shoe! Reuben was drunk, Ned. He would never ride a horse without a shoe unless he was drunk.'

Ned took Smith's body back in the carriage, and Robert tied his handkerchief round my foot and led me slowly home. No one blamed me for the accident. The owner of the White Lion hotel said that Reuben Smith was drunk when he left.

But I had to leave Earlshall, and so did Ginger.

For a month or two I was allowed to live out in a field, and one day Ginger was brought in to join me. She had been ruined by the hard riding of Lord Gray's son, and after twelve months' rest she was going to be sold. And although my knees got better, they looked very ugly and so I was no longer suitable for a fashionable family. It was very pleasant being in the field with Ginger, but one day Robert came in and took me away. We were both very sad to say goodbye to each other, Ginger and I.

I was sold to a man in Bath who kept many horses and different kinds of carriages for hire. I was a 'job horse' and all kinds of people hired me. Some were good drivers, others were very bad. Then one man persuaded my master to sell me to a friend of his who wanted a safe, pleasant horse for riding.

And so that summer I was sold to Mr Barry.

Mr Barry knew very little about horses but he hired a comfortable stable for me, and a man called Filcher to look after me. He ordered the best oats, and plenty of other good food for me to eat, too.

For a while all went well, but then there seemed to be fewer oats and more grass in my meals. The grass food, though very good, was not enough to keep me strong and healthy. However, I could not say anything and it went on for about two months.

Then one afternoon my master rode into the country to see a friend – a gentleman farmer who knew about horses, and who looked very closely at me.

'Your horse doesn't look as well as he did when you first had him, Barry,' he said, feeling my neck and shoulders. 'See how wet and warm he is – after just a gentle ride!'

'My groom says that horses are never in good condition in the autumn,' said my master.

'But this is only August!' said the farmer. 'With your light work and the good food, he shouldn't be like this. I don't know who eats your oats, my friend,' he went on, 'but I doubt that your horse gets any of them. I advise you to watch your groom more closely.'

Oh, how I wanted to speak! I wanted to tell my master where his oats went to. My groom came every morning at six o'clock, bringing his little boy with him. The boy carried a basket and went into the room where the oats were kept. I would see them filling a bag with oats and putting the bag into the basket.

Five or six mornings after the visit to the farmer, the boy left the stable with his basket of oats, but came back soon after, looking frightened, with two policemen holding his arms.

'Show me where your father keeps the food for his chickens,' one policeman said to the boy.

The boy came back with two policemen holding his arms.

The boy began to cry but there was no escape. Moments later, the policemen found another empty bag like the one in the boy's basket, and they took Filcher away with them. That was the last I ever saw of him.

Another groom was employed, but he was very lazy about cleaning and I became thin and unhealthy from standing in a wet, dirty stable. After all this trouble with grooms, Mr Barry decided to stop keeping a horse and I was sent to a horse fair – a place where hundreds of horses were bought and sold, and more lies were told, I think, than in any other place in the country.

That day I was lucky. I was bought for twenty-five pounds by a man called Jeremiah Barker, but everyone called him Jerry and I shall do the same.

10

A London cab horse

Jerry Barker was a small man, but well-made and quick in all his movements. He lived in London and was a cab driver. Jerry's wife, Polly, was a little woman with smooth dark hair and dark eyes. His son, Harry, was nearly twelve years old, and was a tall, good-tempered boy. His daughter, Dolly, was eight, and she looked just like her mother.

Jerry had his own cab and two horses, which he drove and groomed himself. His other horse was a tall, white animal called Captain. The next morning, Polly and Dolly came to see me. Harry had helped his father since early that morning and had already decided that I would be a good horse. Polly brought me a piece of apple and Dolly brought me some bread.

'We'll call him Jack, after the old one,' said Jerry. 'Shall we, Polly?'

'Yes,' she said. 'I like to keep a good name going.'

Captain went out in the cab all morning and I went out in the afternoon. Jerry took a lot of care to make sure that my collar and bridle were comfortable – and there was no bearing rein!

We went to the cab stand where the other cabs were waiting for passengers, and took our place at the back of the last cab. Several of the other drivers came to look at me.

'Too handsome,' said one. 'You'll find something wrong with him one morning.'

Then a man in a grey coat and grey hat came up. His name was Grant, and he looked a happy, sensible kind of man. He had been longer on the cab stand than any of the other men, so they let him through to have a look at me, and waited for his opinion.

He looked me all over very carefully, then said:

'He's the right kind for you, Jerry. I don't care what you paid for him, he'll be worth it.'

My first week as a cab horse was very hard. I was not used to London – the noise, the hurry, the crowds of horses, carts and carriages. But Jerry was a good driver and soon discovered that I was willing to work and do my best. He never used the whip on me, and we soon understood each other as well as a horse and man can do. Jerry kept his horses clean and gave us plenty of food and fresh water, and on Sundays we rested.

I never knew a better man than my new master. He was kind and good-tempered, like John Manly. Harry was clever at stable work and always wanted to do what he could. Polly and Dolly came in the morning to brush out the cab, and to wash the glass, while Jerry gave Captain and me a grooming. There was a lot of laughing and fun between them, which all helped to keep Captain and me happy.

The family came early in the morning because Jerry did not like lateness. It always made him angry when people

*Polly and Dolly cleaned the cab, while Jerry gave
Captain and me a grooming.*

wanted him to drive hard because of their own lateness.

One day, two wild-looking young men called to him.

'Cabby! Hurry up, we're late for our train at Victoria.
Get us there in time for the one o'clock train and we'll pay
you double!'

53

'I will take you at the usual speed, gentlemen,' said Jerry. 'Extra money doesn't pay for extra speed.'

Larry's cab was standing next to ours. He opened the door and said, 'I'm your man, gentlemen! My horse will get you there all right.' And as he shut them in, with a smile at Jerry, he said, 'He always refuses to go faster than a trot!' Then, whipping his horse hard, he went off as fast as he could.

Jerry patted me on the neck. 'Extra money won't pay for that kind of thing, will it, Jack?' he said.

Although he was against hard driving to please careless people, he always went at a fair speed and was not against going faster if there was a good reason.

I remember one morning we were on the stand waiting for a passenger when a young man carrying a large suitcase went by. He stepped on a piece of apple which lay in the road, and fell down heavily. Jerry ran across the road and helped him up, then took him into a shop to sit him down.

Some time later, the young man, looking white and ill, came out again and called Jerry, so we went across the road.

'Can you take me to the South-Eastern Railway?' he said. 'My fall has made me late, and it's very important that I don't miss the twelve o'clock train. I'll pay you extra if you can get me there in time.'

'We'll do our best, sir,' said Jerry, and helped him into the cab.

It was always difficult to drive fast in the city in the

middle of the day, when the streets were full of traffic, but Jerry and I were used to it, and no one was faster at getting through the carriages and carts, all moving at different speeds, going this way and that way. In and out, in and out we went, as fast as a horse can do it. And we got to the station just as the big clock showed eight minutes to twelve.

'We're in time!' said the young man, happily. 'Thank you, my friend, and your good horse, too. Take this extra money—'

'No, sir,' said Jerry. 'Thank you, but it isn't necessary. I'm glad we were in time – now hurry and catch your train.'

When we got back to the cab stand, the other men were laughing because Jerry had driven hard to the train.

'How much extra did he pay you, Jerry?' said one driver.

'Nothing,' said Jerry. 'He offered me extra but I didn't take it. If Jack and I choose to have a quick run now and then, that's our business and not yours.'

'You'll never be a rich man then,' said Larry.

'Perhaps not,' said Jerry, 'but I'll be a happy one!'

'And you, Larry,' added Mr Grant, 'will die poor, because you spend too much money on new whips, beating your poor horse until it's exhausted – and then you have to buy another one.'

'Well, I've never had good luck with my horses,' said Larry.

'And you never will,' said Mr Grant. 'Good Luck is very careful who she travels with, and mostly chooses those who are kind and sensible. That's my experience, anyway.'

He turned round again to his newspaper, and the other men went back to their cabs.

* * *

Winter came early, with snow, rain or strong winds almost every day for weeks. Jerry sometimes went to a coffee-shop near the cab stand, and sometimes Dolly came with some hot soup that Polly had made for him.

One cold windy day, Dolly was waiting for Jerry to finish his soup when a gentleman came towards us. Jerry started to give the soup bowl back to Dolly and was just going to take off my warm cloth when the man said, 'No, no, finish your soup, my friend. I can wait in the cab until you've finished.' Jerry thanked him, then came back to Dolly.

'That's a real gentleman, Dolly,' he said. 'He has time and thought for the comfort of a poor cab driver.'

Jerry finished his soup, then we took the man to Clapham. After that, he took our cab several times, and often came to pat me. It was very unusual for anyone to notice a cab horse, and I was grateful.

Another day, the gentleman saw a cart with two horses standing in the street. The driver was not with them and I don't know how long they had been standing there. However, they decided to move on a few steps.

Suddenly, the cart driver ran out of a building and caught them. He seemed very angry and began to whip the horses hard, even beating them around the head.

Our gentleman saw him and walked quickly across. 'Stop that at once, or I'll call the police!' he said.

The driver was drunk and he began to shout, but he stopped whipping the horses. Meanwhile, our gentleman wrote down the name and address that was on the side of the cart.

'Why do you want that?' shouted the driver.

Our gentleman didn't answer. He came back to the cab. 'Many people have thanked me for telling them how their horses have been used,' he told Jerry.

'I wish there were more gentlemen like you, sir,' said Jerry. 'They're needed in this city.'

— *11* —

Goodbye to old friends

One day we were waiting outside one of the London parks when a dirty old cab drove up beside ours. The horse was brown, with bones that showed through her coat. I was eating some hay and the wind took a little of it her way. The poor animal put out her long thin neck and picked it up, then turned and looked for more. There was a hopeless look in her dull eye and I wondered where I'd seen her before. Then she looked straight at me.

'Black Beauty, is that you?' she said.

It was Ginger! But how different she looked! Her face, which was once so full of life, was now miserable and full of pain, and her breathing was very bad.

I moved closer to her so that we could have a quiet talk, and it was a sad story that she told me. After twelve months' rest at Earlshall she was considered to be ready to work again, and was sold to a gentleman. She got on well for a little while, but after a long gallop one day, she became

It was Ginger! But how different she looked!

ill again. She was rested, was seen by a horse-doctor, then sold. In this way, she went from owner to owner several times, each one poorer than the one before.

'So at last I was bought by a man who keeps a number of cabs and horses, and hires them out,' said Ginger. 'You look happy and comfortable with life as a cab horse, and I'm glad, but it's different for me. They whip me and work me seven days a week. They say that they paid more for me than I was worth, and now they're trying to get their money back by working me until I drop.'

'You used to stand up and fight when people were cruel to you,' I said.

'Yes, I did once,' said Ginger. 'But men are stronger than we are, and if they're cruel and have no feelings, then there's nothing we can do about it. Oh, I wish the end would come. I wish I was dead.'

I was very sad. I put my nose against hers but could find nothing to say that would cheer her up. I think she was pleased to see me, because she said, 'You're the only friend I ever had.'

A few weeks after this, a cart with a dead horse in it passed by our cab stand. It was a brown horse with a long thin neck, and I believe it was Ginger. I hoped it was, because then her troubles would be over.

* * *

There was one day when we were very busy. First a fat gentleman with a large bag wanted to go to Bishopsgate Station; then we were called by a lady who wanted to be taken to Regent's Park; then a man jumped into the cab and called out, 'Bow Street Police Station, quick!'

After another journey or two, we came back to the cab stand and Jerry gave me some food, saying, 'We must eat when we can on days like this, Jack.' And he took out the meat and bread Polly had given him.

But neither of us had eaten many mouthfuls before a poor young woman came along the street. She was carrying a child and she looked lost and worried.

'Can you tell me the way to St Thomas's Hospital, please?' she asked. 'I have to take my little boy there, and I'm a stranger in London.' The little boy was crying as she spoke. 'He's in great pain and can't walk, but the doctor says that if I can get him to the hospital, then perhaps he'll get well again.'

'You can't carry him through the crowds,' said Jerry. 'It's five kilometres, and that child is heavy.'

'I'm strong,' said the woman. 'I think I can manage, if I know the way.'

'You can't do it. Just get into this cab and I'll drive you there. Don't you see that it's beginning to rain?'

'No, sir, I can't do that,' she said. 'I've only just enough money to get me home again.'

'Listen,' said Jerry. 'I've got a wife and children at home, and I'd be ashamed of myself if I let a woman and a sick child put themselves in danger. Get in the cab and I'll take you for nothing.'

'Oh, how kind you are!' said the woman, and began to cry.

Jerry opened the door but two men ran up, calling out, 'Cab!'

'It's taken,' said Jerry, but one man pushed past the woman and jumped in, followed by the other. 'This cab is already taken, gentlemen,' Jerry said again, 'by this lady.'

'Lady!' said one of the men unpleasantly, looking at the woman's poor clothes. 'She can wait. Our business is very important, and anyway, we were in first, and we'll stay in.'

A smile came over Jerry's face as he shut the cab door. 'Stay in as long as you like, gentlemen. I can wait while you rest yourselves.' He walked over to the young woman who was standing nearby. 'They'll soon be gone, don't worry,' he said, laughing.

And he was right. When the two men realized that they were going to have a very long wait, they got out, calling Jerry all kinds of bad names. After this, we were soon on our way to the hospital.

'Thank you a thousand times,' said the young woman, as Jerry helped her out of the cab.

'I hope your child will soon be better,' said Jerry. He watched her go in, then patted my neck. It was something he always did when he was pleased.

The rain was now coming down fast and, just as we were leaving the hospital, a lady came down the steps calling, 'Cab!' Jerry seemed to know her at once.

'Jerry Barker, is it you?' said the woman. 'I'm very glad to find you here. It's difficult to get a cab in this part of London today.'

The two men called Jerry all kinds of bad names.

'I'll be proud to take you,' said Jerry. 'Where do you want to go?'

'Paddington Station,' said the woman.

We got to the station and went in under cover. The lady stood beside the cab talking to Jerry for some time, and I discovered that she was once Polly's mistress.

'How do you like cab work in the winter?' she asked Jerry. 'Polly was worried about your cough last year.'

'She worries because I work all hours and in all kinds of

weather,' said Jerry. 'But I get on all right, and I would be lost without horses to look after.'

'It would be wrong to harm your health in this work when you have a wife and two children,' said the lady. 'There are many places where good drivers or grooms are wanted. If you ever decide to give up cab work, let me know.' She put something into his hand. 'There's some money for the children.'

Jerry thanked her and, after leaving the station, we went home.

* * *

Christmas and the New Year are no holidays for cab drivers and their horses. People go to parties and dances, and the work is often late. Sometimes driver and horse have to wait for hours, shaking with cold.

We had a lot of late work during Christmas week and Jerry's cough was bad. On New Year's Eve we took two gentlemen to a house in the West End, and were told to come for them at eleven o'clock. 'You may have to wait a few minutes, but don't be late,' one of them said.

Jerry arrived at the right time and we waited. The wind was very cold and it was snowing. Jerry pulled one of my cloths higher over my neck, then walked up and down, trying to keep warm.

At half-past twelve, Jerry rang the door-bell and asked if the gentlemen still wanted the cab. The man at the door said, 'Oh, yes, you'll be wanted.'

At one o'clock the door opened and two men came out.

They got in the cab without a word, and told Jerry where to drive. It was three kilometres away, and when the men got out they didn't say they were sorry for the long wait, but they were angry when Jerry made them pay for the extra waiting time. But it was money hard-earned.

When we got home, Jerry could not speak, and his cough was terrible, but he groomed me and made sure that I was warm and comfortable.

It was late the next morning before anyone came, and then it was only Harry. He cleaned us and gave us our food but was very quiet. Later that morning he came again, and this time Dolly came with him. She was crying, and I discovered from their conversation that Jerry was dangerously ill.

Two days passed, and only Harry and Dolly came to the stable. On the third day, Mr Grant from the cab stand arrived when Harry was in the stable. 'I won't go to the house, boy, but how is your father?' he said.

'He's very bad,' said Harry.

'I'm sorry to hear that,' said Mr Grant. 'He's the best man I know.'

But when he came the next day, Harry was able to tell him, 'Father is better today. Mother hopes he will get over it soon.'

'Thank God!' said Mr Grant. He was a kind man, and did a lot to help the family during this time, because while Jerry was ill, he was earning no money, and we all had to eat.

Jerry got slowly better, but the doctor said he must never do cab work again. The children talked a lot about what their mother and father would do, but a few days later Dolly ran into the stable to find Harry.

'There's a letter from Mrs Fowler, mother's old mistress!' said Dolly. 'She wants father to be her carriage driver, and we're going to live in a cottage in the country – with chickens, and apple trees, and everything!'

This was bad news for me. I was not young now, and could not hope for a better master than Jerry, although Mr Grant promised to find a comfortable place for me.

I never saw Jerry again and was very sorry to leave.

— *12* —

Hard times

I was sold to a baker who Jerry knew, but the baker's cart driver was a man called Jakes, who drove with the bearing rein up. This made it difficult for me to pull a heavy cart, and I found the work very hard.

One day, after three or four months of this, I was pulling the cart, which was much heavier than usual, up a steep hill. I had to stop several times to rest, which didn't please Jakes.

'Move on, you lazy horse, or I'll make you!' he shouted, and he hit me with his whip.

After a few more metres, I had to stop again. The whip came down across my back once more and the pain was sharp. I was doing my best but the driver was still punishing me cruelly, which seemed very unfair.

Jakes was whipping me a third time when a woman hurried over and said, 'Oh, please don't whip your horse like that. I think I can help, if you'll let me.'

Jakes laughed. 'Oh?'

'He can't use all his strength when his head is held back with that bearing rein,' the woman went on. 'If you take it off, I'm sure he'll do better.'

'Anything to please a lady,' said Jakes, smiling.

The rein was taken off and I moved my head up and down several times to help my aching neck.

'Poor boy, is that what you wanted?' said the woman, patting me. She turned to Jakes. 'If you speak to him kindly and lead him on, I believe he'll do better.'

Jakes took the rein, and I put down my head and moved on. I pulled the cart up the hill, then stopped to take a breath.

'Well, that helped,' said Jakes, 'but if I went without a bearing rein all the time, the other cart drivers would laugh at me. It's fashionable, you see.'

'It's better to start a good fashion than to follow a bad one,' said the woman. 'Many gentlemen don't use bearing reins now.'

She gave me another pat on the neck and walked on.

After that, Jakes always took off my bearing rein when I

was going up a hill, and that made my life easier. But pulling heavy carts day after day slowly began to exhaust me and a younger horse was brought in to do my work.

* * *

I was sold to another cab owner whose name was Nicholas Skinner. He was hard on his drivers, and they were hard on the horses. We worked long hours, had no Sunday rest, and it was a hot summer.

My driver was just as hard as his master, and he had a cruel whip with something sharp at the end which often cut me and made me bleed. It was a terrible life, and sometimes, like poor Ginger, I wished I was dead.

One day I nearly got my wish.

We were at the railway station when a family of four people hired us. There was a noisy man with a lady, a little boy, a young girl, and a lot of heavy luggage.

'Father,' said the young girl, 'this poor horse can't take us *and* all our luggage. He's too tired.'

'Oh, he's all right, miss!' said my driver. He put a heavy box on the cab with the other luggage.

'Father, please take a second cab,' said the girl. 'I'm sure this is very cruel.'

'Grace, get in at once, and don't be stupid,' said her father. 'The driver knows his own business.'

My gentle friend had to obey, and box after box was lifted up and put on the top of the cab, or next to the driver. Then the driver hit me with his whip and we moved out of the station.

The cab was very heavy and I had not eaten or rested since early that morning. I did my best and got along quite well until we came to Ludgate Hill. By then I was exhausted, and the heavy cab was too much for me. My feet went from under me and I fell heavily, knocking all the breath out of me. I lay quite still because I could not move. Indeed, I expected to die.

There were angry voices above me and luggage was taken off the cab, but it was all like a dream. I thought I heard the girl's voice saying, 'Oh, that poor horse! It's all our fault!'

Someone loosened my bridle and collar, and another voice said, 'He's dead, he'll never get up again.' I heard a policeman giving orders but I did not open my eyes. Cold water was thrown over my head, some medicine was put into my mouth, and I was covered with a cloth.

I don't know how long I was there, but a man with a kind voice persuaded me to try to get up – and I managed it. Then I was gently led to some stables close by.

That evening, I was taken back to Skinner's stables, and the next morning the horse-doctor came to see me.

'He's been worked too hard,' said the doctor. 'There's no strength left in him.'

'Then he must go for dog food,' said Skinner. 'I have no fields for sick horses. It doesn't suit my business. I work them for as long as they'll go, then I sell them for what I can get.'

'There's a horse fair in ten days' time,' said the doctor. 'If

I heard the girl's voice saying, 'Oh, that poor horse!
It's all our fault!

you rest him and give him food, he may get better, and then you may get more than his skin's worth.'

Luckily for me, Skinner took the doctor's advice and, after rest and food, I began to feel better. Ten days later, I was taken to the horse fair, a few miles outside London.

— *13* —

My last home

I was sold to a farmer at the horse fair, but it was his young grandson who persuaded him to buy me.

The two of them walked past me and, seeing kindness in the farmer's face, I lifted my head, put my ears forward and tried to look my best.

The farmer stopped and looked at me. 'There's a horse, Willie, that has known better days,' he said.

'Poor thing!' said the boy. 'Do you think he was ever a carriage horse, grandfather?'

'Oh, yes,' said the farmer. 'Look at his fine head and the shape of his neck and shoulder.' He reached out a hand and patted me on the neck. I put out my nose in answer to his kindness, and the boy gently put his hand against my face.

'Look how well he understands kindness,' said the boy. 'Won't you buy him, and make him young and strong again?'

The man who was selling me said, 'The boy can recognize

a good horse, sir. This one isn't old, just tired and thin from too much work. In six months, he'll be fine.'

Five pounds changed hands and, soon after, I was taken to my new home. The farmer gave orders for me to have hay and oats every night and morning, and I was let out into a large field in the daytime. Willie, the young boy, was responsible for me, and he came to see me every day, bringing carrots or apples.

During that winter, the rest, the good food, the soft grass and gentle running and trotting all helped to make me feel quite young again. When the spring came, the farmer tried me with a carriage, and I did the work quite easily.

'He's growing young, Willie,' he said. 'We'll give him some gentle work and look for a good home for him.'

* * *

One day during this summer, the groom cleaned and dressed me with special care, and Willie seemed half-worried and half-excited as he got into the carriage with his grandfather.

'I hope the ladies like him,' said the farmer.

A kilometre or two beyond the village, we came to a pretty house, and Willie went to knock on the door. He asked if Miss Blomefield and Miss Ellen were at home. They were, and Willie stayed with me while the farmer went into the house. He came back about ten minutes later with three ladies. They seemed to like me, but one of them, worried by my knees, wondered if I was safe.

'It's true his knees were broken once,' said the farmer,

'but we don't know why he fell. It was probably a careless driver, and not the horse's fault at all. He seems very safe to me. If you like him, you can try him for a few weeks,' he went on. 'Then your driver will see what he thinks of him.'

One of the three ladies – a tall, white-faced lady, who held the arm of a younger woman – said, 'You have always given us good advice about our horses, so we accept your offer to try him.'

The next morning, a young man came for me. He looked pleased until he saw my knees, then he said, 'I'm surprised you suggested this horse to my ladies.'

'You're only taking him to try him,' said the farmer. 'If he's not as safe as any horse you ever drove, send him back, young man.'

I was taken to a comfortable stable, given some food, then left to myself.

The next day, the groom was cleaning my face when he said, 'That's just like the star that Black Beauty had on his forehead. I wonder where he is now.' He looked more closely at me. 'White star on the forehead, one white foot – and a little white place on his back! It must be Black Beauty! Beauty! Do you know me? I'm little Joe Green, who almost killed you!' And he began patting me all over my back.

I could not say I remembered him, as he was now a fine young man with a black moustache and a deep voice. But I was sure he knew me, and that he was Joe Green, and I was very glad. I put my nose up to him and tried to say that we were friends. I never saw a man so pleased.

That afternoon, I was harnessed to a carriage for Miss Ellen to try me. Joe Green went with her and told her that he was sure I was Mr Gordon's old Black Beauty.

'I shall write to Mrs Gordon and tell her that her favourite horse has come to us,' said Miss Ellen. 'How pleased she will be!'

I have now lived in this happy place a whole year. Joe is the best and kindest of grooms. My work is easy and pleasant, and I feel my strength coming back again.

The ladies have promised that they will never sell me, and so I have nothing to fear; and here my story ends. My troubles are all over, and I am at home; and often, before I am quite awake, I dream I am still in the field at Birtwick, standing with my old friends under the apple trees.

My troubles are all over, and I am at home.

73

GLOSSARY

cab   a taxi

cough *(v)*   to push out air violently and noisily from the throat

dealer   someone who buys and sells things

drunk *(adj)*   feeling the effects of too much alcoholic drink

feed *(v)*   to give food to a person or animal, or to eat something

gallop   (of a horse) to run very fast

groom *(n)*   a person whose job is to look after horses in a stable

groom *(v)*   to clean and brush a horse's coat

harness *(n)*   the straps, collar, etc. on a horse's head and body which fasten the horse to a carriage

harness *(v)*   to fasten a horse to a carriage with straps

hay   dried grass, which is used to feed animals

hunt *(v and n)*   to chase and kill animals for food or sport

look after   to take care of something or someone

mare   an adult female horse

master/mistress   a man/woman who owns animals and employs people to look after them

neigh *(n)*   the loud cry of a horse

oats   a kind of plant used as food (for animals and people)

pat *(v)*   to touch gently with your hand several times

pleasant   nice, enjoyable, pleasing

race *(n)*   a competition to see who can run, ride, etc. the fastest

ruin *(v)*   to harm or damage something completely

strength   being strong

temper   how you feel (e.g. a bad-tempered person is angry)

tight   fixed or fastened very closely

treat   to behave well or badly towards someone or something

trot   (of a horse) to run slowly, with short steps

Black Beauty

ACTIVITIES

Before Reading

1 **Read the story introduction on the first page of the book, and the back cover. What do you know now about the story? Answer these questions.**

1 Who is telling the story?
2 What were the first four years of Black Beauty's life like?
3 What have you learnt about his training and character?
4 How were horses treated in the 1870s?

2 **Can you guess what kind of work Black Beauty has to do in his life? Choose some of these ideas.**

1 He carries riders.
2 He works on a farm.
3 He pulls a fire-engine.
4 He pulls a taxi-cab.
5 He pulls carriages.
6 He pulls a baker's cart.
7 He goes hunting.
8 He runs in horse races.

3 **Can you guess what happens to Black Beauty in the story? Choose Y (Yes) or N (No) for each sentence.**

1 He falls when galloping, and breaks his knees. Y/N
2 He wins an important race, and then is stolen. Y/N
3 He has to work so hard that he nearly dies. Y/N
4 A groom saves his life in a stable fire. Y/N
5 He is beaten by his master, and is sold for dog food. Y/N
6 He returns to his first home, and dies in peace. Y/N

ACTIVITIES

While Reading

Read Chapters 1 and 2. Complete this passage about Black Beauty with words from the story. Use one word in each gap.

Until he was _____ years old, Black Beauty lived in a _____ and was able to _____ around with other young horses. Then he began his training. He had to learn to wear a _____ on his back and a bridle on his _____, with a cold metal bit in his _____. When he pulled a _____ behind him, he had to wear a heavy _____ on his neck and blinkers against his _____.

He was lucky with his next home. He lived in a pleasant _____ with Merrylegs, a fat little _____, and Ginger, a tall brown _____. His new master, John the _____, and James the stableboy were all _____ people.

Read Chapters 3 to 5. Who said this, and to whom? What or who were they talking about?

1 'A bad-tempered man will never make a good-tempered horse.'
2 'Kindness is all she needs, poor thing.'
3 'It was the only thing they could understand.'
4 'At that time, some owners thought it was fashionable.'
5 'He's not supposed to turn in through your gates.'
6 'Black Beauty was cleverer than we were.'
7 'He doesn't have much experience of driving, but he has a light touch and a quick eye.'

Before you read Chapter 6 (*The fire*), can you guess what will happen in this chapter?

1 Where will the fire be, and who will be in danger?
2 What will happen to Black Beauty in the fire?
3 What kind of person will James show himself to be?

Read Chapters 6 to 8. Choose the best question-word for these questions, and then answer them.

What / Why

1 . . . was Dick Towler doing in the stable at the hotel?
2 . . . couldn't Black Beauty breathe when he woke up?
3 . . . did James tie a scarf over Black Beauty's eyes?
4 . . . did Joe Green do wrong after Black Beauty's ride for
    the doctor?
5 . . . was Joe heart-broken after this?
6 . . . did Joe shout at the man with the brick-cart?
7 . . . did Lady Gray want York to do to her carriage horses?
8 . . . made Ginger kick herself out of the carriage one day?
9 . . . did Black Beauty do when Lady Anne had an accident?

Before you read Chapter 9 (*The accident and new masters*), what do you think is going to happen? Circle Y (Yes) or N (No) for each of these possibilities.

Black Beauty . . .

1 is badly injured when another horse kicks him. Y/N
2 falls and hurts his knees while carrying a drunk rider. Y/N
3 breaks a leg while jumping a ditch. Y/N

4 falls, and his rider is thrown off and killed. Y/N
5 is wrongly blamed for the accident. Y/N
6 is given away to a neighbour. Y/N
7 is bought by a man who hires out horses. Y/N
8 is sold to a farmer. Y/N

Read Chapters 9 to 11. Are these questions true (T) or false (F)? Rewrite the false sentences with the correct information.

1 Black Beauty fell because Smith whipped him so hard.
2 Black Beauty was sold because his knees looked ugly.
3 The groom's son stole Black Beauty's oats and ate them.
4 Jerry Barker did not bother to take care of his horses.
5 Ginger's life as a cab horse was much harder than Black Beauty's.
6 Jerry liked to help people who were in trouble.
7 When Jerry got a new job in the country, Mr Grant bought Black Beauty.

Before you read Chapters 12 and 13 (*Hard times* and *My last home*), can you guess how the story will end?

1 Who will buy Black Beauty next, and how will his new masters treat him?
2 How will he feel, as he gets older and weaker, and has to work harder? Will he hate people who are cruel to him, or just accept the way some humans behave to animals?
3 What will his 'last home' be like? Will he find peace at last, in a quiet field, with a kind master or mistress? Or will he be glad to die, like Ginger, and escape from a hard life?

After Reading

1 Here is a list of Black Beauty's owners. Match them with the kinds of work that they made Black Beauty do. (Some kinds of work will be needed more than once.)

carrying a rider / light work / pulling a delivery cart / pulling a cab / pulling a carriage

1 Nicholas Skinner
2 Lord and Lady Gray
3 The Blomefield family
4 Mr Barry
5 A baker
6 Mr Gordon
7 A farmer
8 A man from Bath
9 Jerry Barker

Put the owners in the order in which they appear in the story, and then write a short description of them and how they treated Black Beauty.

2 After the fire (page 30), James probably told John all about it. Complete James' side of their conversation.

JOHN: When did the fire start?
JAMES: _____
JOHN: And how bad was it when you got there?
JAMES: _____
JOHN: I expect it was hard to get the horses out.
JAMES: _____

JOHN: Did anyone find out how the fire started?

JAMES: _____

JOHN: Anyway, you did really well to save our horses. The
master's very pleased with you.

3 **When Ginger kicked herself out of the carriage, Lord Gray
asked York what had happened (see page 41). Put their
conversation in the right order, and write in the speakers'
names. Begin with number 3.**

1 _____ 'Women don't understand horses, York! In future
take orders only from me, not from my wife.'

2 _____ 'I think the bearing rein was too tight for her, sir.'

3 _____ 'Now tell me exactly what happened, York.'

4 _____ 'Her ladyship asked me to make it tighter, sir.'

5 _____ 'But what made Ginger behave so badly?'

6 _____ 'I'm afraid we lost control of Ginger, my lord, and
had to cut the horses out of the harness.'

7 _____ 'No, better not. Put another horse in next time.'

8 _____ 'Right, sir. Shall I try Ginger in the carriage again?'

9 _____ 'Well, why *was* the bearing rein so tight?'

4 **Do you agree (A) or disagree (D) with these ideas? Give your
reasons.**

1 A motor car is a much better kind of transport than a
horse and carriage.

2 For humans, a horse is the most useful of all animals.

3 It is cruel to make a horse pull a carriage or carry a rider
on his back.

5 There are 27 words (4 letters or longer) from the story in this word search. Find the words (they go from left to right, and from top to bottom), and draw lines through them.

C	F	R	E	E	D	O	M	R	M	A	R	E	U
T	I	G	H	T	E	L	F	A	S	H	I	O	N
T	E	Y	H	R	I	G	S	C	A	H	D	M	E
T	L	V	A	E	E	A	G	A	D	O	E	A	R
E	D	B	R	I	D	L	E	R	D	O	R	S	Y
M	G	T	N	N	W	L	N	R	L	F	B	T	S
P	R	R	E	K	H	O	T	I	E	O	D	E	T
E	A	E	S	I	I	P	L	A	T	Y	P	R	A
R	S	A	S	C	P	S	E	G	R	O	O	M	B
B	S	T	U	K	R	A	C	E	O	S	N	I	L
N	R	U	I	N	E	C	A	R	T	S	Y	S	E

6 Now use 13 words from the word search to complete this passage.

'How I wish I could live in a _____, not a _____! Never to wear _____ again or to pull a _____ behind me! To feel soft _____ under my feet, and to have the _____ to _____ where I want, without a heavy _____ on my back! Why do humans _____ us so badly? They care more about _____ than about us. Oh no, she wants the bearing _____ shorter today. I can see how _____ he's made it on Beauty. No, I won't have it! I'm going to _____ my way out of this . . .'

Which horse is thinking this, where is the horse, and what is just about to happen?

82

7 **Look at the word search again, and write down all the letters without a line through them. Begin with the first line, and go across each line to the end. You should have 27 letters, which will make a sentence of 4 words.**

  1 What is the sentence, and who said it, to whom?

  2 What had just happened that caused the speaker to say it?

  3 Do you agree or disagree with the sentence? Why?

8 **Here are some quotes from the story. What was the speaker talking about, and what did it show about his or her feelings for horses?**

  1 'Men may be clever enough to think of things for themselves, but animals know things *without* thinking.' (Mr Gordon, page 24)

  2 'Stupid boy! No cloth put on, and I suppose the water was cold too.' (John Manly, page 34)

  3 'The wheels are half-buried and won't move. I'll help you take some bricks out to make the cart lighter.' (Joe Green, page 35)

  4 'York, you must put those horses' heads higher; they don't look nice.' (Lady Gray, page 39)

  5 'I don't know who eats your oats, my friend, but I doubt that your horse gets any of them.' (a gentleman farmer, page 49)

  6 'It's better to start a good fashion than to follow a bad one.' (a woman passer-by, page 66)

  7 'I have no fields for sick horses. It doesn't suit my business.' (Nicholas Skinner, page 68)

ABOUT THE AUTHOR

Anna Sewell was born in 1820 in Great Yarmouth, in the east of England. She lived a quiet life with her family in the country. Her mother wrote poems and stories for children, and Anna sometimes helped with the writing, by reading the stories and suggesting changes. When Anna was young, she had an accident which made it hard for her to walk, and in later years she could only get about in a pony-cart. By the time she was fifty, her health had got much worse, and she no longer left the house.

In order to pass the time, she started writing a story about a horse. This is what she said: 'I have for six years been confined to the house and to my sofa, and have from time to time, as I was able, been writing what I think will turn out a little book, its special aim being to induce kindness, sympathy, and an understanding treatment of horses.' She had always loved animals, especially horses, and hated hearing about or seeing people's cruelty towards horses. The character of Black Beauty was based on her brother's horse, Bessie, who was a great favourite with the family.

Black Beauty, Anna Sewell's only novel, was published in 1877, only a few months before she died in 1878, so she never knew what a huge success it became. By 1935 it had sold more than twenty million copies throughout the world, and it is probably the most famous story about horses ever written. It has been filmed five times; the most recent film, in 1994, is the first one in which the story is told by Black Beauty himself, just as in the original book.

OXFORD BOOKWORMS LIBRARY

Classics • Crime & Mystery • Factfiles • Fantasy & Horror
Human Interest • Playscripts • Thriller & Adventure
True Stories • World Stories

The OXFORD BOOKWORMS LIBRARY provides enjoyable reading in English, with a wide range of classic and modern fiction, non-fiction, and plays. It includes original and adapted texts in seven carefully graded language stages, which take learners from beginner to advanced level. An overview is given on the next pages.

All Stage 1 titles are available as audio recordings, as well as over eighty other titles from Starter to Stage 6. All Starters and many titles at Stages 1 to 4 are specially recommended for younger learners. Every Bookworm is illustrated, and Starters and Factfiles have full-colour illustrations.

The OXFORD BOOKWORMS LIBRARY also offers extensive support. Each book contains an introduction to the story, notes about the author, a glossary, and activities. Additional resources include tests and worksheets, and answers for these and for the activities in the books. There is advice on running a class library, using audio recordings, and the many ways of using Oxford Bookworms in reading programmes. Resource materials are available on the website <www.oup.com/elt/bookworms>.

The *Oxford Bookworms Collection* is a series for advanced learners. It consists of volumes of short stories by well-known authors, both classic and modern. Texts are not abridged or adapted in any way, but carefully selected to be accessible to the advanced student.

You can find details and a full list of titles in the *Oxford Bookworms Library Catalogue* and *Oxford English Language Teaching Catalogues*, and on the website <www.oup.com/elt/bookworms>.

THE OXFORD BOOKWORMS LIBRARY
GRADING AND SAMPLE EXTRACTS

STARTER • 250 HEADWORDS

present simple – present continuous – imperative –
can/cannot, must – *going to* (future) – simple gerunds …

Her phone is ringing – but where is it?

Sally gets out of bed and looks in her bag. No phone. She looks under the bed. No phone. Then she looks behind the door. There is her phone. Sally picks up her phone and answers it. *Sally's Phone*

STAGE 1 • 400 HEADWORDS

… past simple – coordination with *and*, *but*, *or* –
subordination with *before*, *after*, *when*, *because*, *so* …

I knew him in Persia. He was a famous builder and I worked with him there. For a time I was his friend, but not for long. When he came to Paris, I came after him – I wanted to watch him. He was a very clever, very dangerous man. *The Phantom of the Opera*

STAGE 2 • 700 HEADWORDS

… present perfect – *will* (future) – *(don't) have to, must not, could* –
comparison of adjectives – simple *if* clauses – past continuous –
tag questions – *ask/tell* + infinitive …

While I was writing these words in my diary, I decided what to do. I must try to escape. I shall try to get down the wall outside. The window is high above the ground, but I have to try. I shall take some of the gold with me – if I escape, perhaps it will be helpful later. *Dracula*

... should, may – present perfect continuous – *used to* – past perfect –
causative – relative clauses – indirect statements ...

Of course, it was most important that no one should see
Colin, Mary, or Dickon entering the secret garden. So Colin
gave orders to the gardeners that they must all keep away
from that part of the garden in future. *The Secret Garden*

STAGE 4 • 1400 HEADWORDS

... past perfect continuous – passive (simple forms) –
would conditional clauses – indirect questions –
relatives with *where/when* – gerunds after prepositions/phrases ...

I was glad. Now Hyde could not show his face to the world
again. If he did, every honest man in London would be proud
to report him to the police. *Dr Jekyll and Mr Hyde*

STAGE 5 • 1800 HEADWORDS

... future continuous – future perfect –
passive (modals, continuous forms) –
would have conditional clauses – modals + perfect infinitive ...

If he had spoken Estella's name, I would have hit him. I was so
angry with him, and so depressed about my future, that I could
not eat the breakfast. Instead I went straight to the old house.
Great Expectations

STAGE 6 • 2500 HEADWORDS

... passive (infinitives, gerunds) – advanced modal meanings –
clauses of concession, condition

When I stepped up to the piano, I was confident. It was as if I
knew that the prodigy side of me really did exist. And when I
started to play, I was so caught up in how lovely I looked that
I didn't worry how I would sound. *The Joy Luck Club*

Little Women

LOUISA MAY ALCOTT

Retold by John Escott

When Christmas comes for the four March girls, there is no money for expensive presents and they give away their Christmas breakfast to a poor family. But there are no happier girls in America than Meg, Jo, Beth, and Amy. They miss their father, of course, who is away at the Civil War, but they try hard to be good so that he will be proud of his 'little women' when he comes home.

This heart-warming story of family life has been popular for more than a hundred years.

The Silver Sword

IAN SERRAILLIER

Retold by John Escott

Jan opened his wooden box and took out the silver sword. 'This will bring me luck,' he said to Mr Balicki. 'And it will bring you luck because you gave it to me.'

The silver sword is only a paper knife, but it gives Jan and his friends hope. Hungry, cold, and afraid, the four children try to stay alive among the ruins of bombed cities in war-torn Europe. Soon they will begin the long and dangerous journey south, from Poland to Switzerland, where they hope to find their parents again.